Published By: Ishwar Pratap Singh Raghuwanshi

Edition: 1st

Published Year: 2026

Title: ATMAVAAD

Beyond Tradition: The Unique Face Of Ayurveda

Author: Dr. Ishwar Pratap Singh Raghuwanshi

Co-authors- Dr. Bhumika Tomar , Dr. Jaishree Soni

Email: dr.ishwar.raghuwanshi@gmail.com

Mobile: +91-9425148235

ISBN: 978-93-5759-296-3

Preface

Atmavaad - Beyond Tradition: The Unique Face of Ayurveda

Ayurveda is not merely a system of medicine; it is a philosophy of life rooted in the understanding of existence itself. Derived from the wisdom of ancient seers and preserved through classical texts such as Charaka Samhita, Sushruta Samhita, and Ashtanga Hridaya, Ayurveda transcends the boundaries of treatment and enters the realm of consciousness, ethics, and self-realization.

The concept of **Atmavaad** reflects this deeper dimension. It signifies the recognition of the *Atma* (self) as the foundation of health, disease, and healing. While modern interpretations often present Ayurveda as a traditional healthcare science, its core is profoundly philosophical-bridging body, mind, and soul in a unified framework.

This book, *Atmavaad -Beyond Tradition*, attempts to explore Ayurveda not only as an ancient discipline but as a timeless science of awareness. It highlights the unique identity of Ayurveda in today's globalized world-where science seeks evidence, yet humanity seeks meaning.

The purpose of this work is to:

- Revisit classical foundations with contemporary clarity
- Present the philosophical essence behind practical applications
- Illustrate Ayurveda as a living science rather than a preserved tradition
- Inspire readers to perceive health as harmony between Sharira, Manas, and Atma

In an era where healthcare often becomes mechanical, Ayurveda reminds us that healing begins with consciousness. The doctrine of Atmavaad encourages us to look beyond symptoms and explore the inner self-the true seat of balance.

This book is dedicated to scholars, practitioners, students, and seekers who wish to understand Ayurveda not just as treatment, but as truth.

May this work serve as a bridge between tradition and transformation.

AUTHOR

Dr. Ishwar Pratap Singh Raghuwanshi.

Special Acknowledgment

(Special Dedication to My Family)

"A book may be the creation of an author, but its seed is sown in the environment where it receives love, inspiration, and support."

I express my heartfelt gratitude to my family, who have nurtured the seed of my life with constant care and strength.

Matrushakti – My mother, whose affection, silent prayers, and selfless love have flowed as an unseen strength in every endeavour of mine. Her emotional support forms the very foundation of my thoughts. She is the primary source of my consciousness.

Pitrushakti – My father, whose ideals of life, discipline, self-respect, and dedication to duty have taught me the lessons of patience, wisdom, and responsibility. In every line of this book, his moral discipline resonates.

Wife – My Ardhangini on the path of life, who shared the ups and downs of my writing journey without a single complaint. Her patience, encouragement, and constant presence have been the cornerstone in the creation of this book. She remains the enduring inspiration behind my creative energy.

Daughter – My little daughter, the gentle inspiration behind my thoughts. Her innocent smile, curious questions, and childlike expressions continuously generate new energy within me. This book is a silent answer to her—that the labor of knowledge can indeed be sweet and fulfilling.

Without these four pillars—Mother, Father, Wife, and Daughter—this book would have remained incomplete. Their selfless love and silent support have flowed as the very soul of my writing.

This work is dedicated to them.

With respect,

Dr. Ishwar Pratap Singh Raghuvanshi

About the Author

Dr. Ishwar Pratap Singh Raghuvanshi completed his Ayurvedacharya in 2011 from Om Ayurved Mahavidyalaya evam Chikitsalaya. He subsequently earned his Postgraduate degree (2021) in Ayurveda Samhita evam Siddhanta from Pt. Khushilal Sharma Government (Autonomous) Ayurveda College and Institute.

He is presently serving as a Lecturer at Rani Dullaiya Smriti Ayurved Mahavidyalaya.

Dr. Raghuwanshi has published 01 Book (O.S.P.E. of Padartha Vijnana) and 06 research papers in UGC Care listed journals and has presented research papers and actively participated in 4 national and international seminars and workshops.

Email: dr.ishwar.raghuwanshi@gmail.com

Contact: +91-9425148235

About the co-author

Dr. Bhumika Tomar and **Dr. Jaishree Soni** are dedicated Postgraduate Scholars from the Department of Samhita Siddhanta at Rani Dullaiya Smriti Ayurved P.G. Mahavidyalaya and Chikitsalaya. Both are actively engaged in advanced academic study and research cantered on the classical principles and philosophical foundations of Ayurveda.

Their specialization in Samhita Siddhanta enables them to approach Ayurvedic texts with deep conceptual understanding, textual sensitivity, and terminological precision. With strong grounding in classical *Granthas* and contemporary academic methodology, they ensure that interpretations maintain originality, authenticity, and conceptual integrity without dilution.

Through their scholarly discipline and commitment to the preservation and propagation of authentic Ayurvedic knowledge, they have significantly contributed to the clarity, depth, and academic strength of this work.

Co-author

Dr. Bhumika Tomar	Dr. Jaishree Soni
+91-9981995472	+91-7974610411
bhumikatomar44@gmail.com	drjaishreesoni@gmail.com

CONTENT

CHAPTER-1

CONCEPT OF PURUSHA

Purusha is the main factor with whom medicine is concerned and as such it has been discussed and defined thoroughly. In *Charak Samhita (Sharira.*1*),* in answer to the question as to how many *Purusha* are there it has been said that *Purusha* is of three types according to components-*Ek Purusha* (pure consciousness), *Shada-dhatvatmaka Purusha* and *Chaturvinshatika Purusha* or *Rashipurusha* having conglomeration of twenty-four principles e.g. *Manas,* Ten *Indriyas, Artha* (sense objects) and *Prakruti* consisting of eight principles *Avyakta, Buddhi, Ahankara* and *Panchabhutas.* The sixteen principles other than *Prakruti* are termed as *'Vikara'.*

Evidently the concept of *Chaturvinshatika* or *Rashipurusha* is the same as in the *Sankhya Darshana* but different from that adopted by *Isvarakrsna* where *Purusha* is the twenty-fifth one apart from the twenty-four principles of *Prakruti* and *Vikara.* The latter one is accepted by *Susruta* but *Charaka* holds the earlier view (probably of *Pancasikha*) according to which the principle of consciousness is not separate but a member of the conglomeration. In *Mahabharata* (*Shanti.*318.72), *Chaturvinshatika Purusha* is mentioned besides *Panchvinshatika* and *Shadvinshatika.* This may be correlated with *Ksara, Aksara* and *Purushottama* of *Gita.* Commenting of the above unmanifested-ness *Purusha* is including in *Prakruti* itself. *Dasgupta* has evolved a novel way by bifurcating *Prakruti* in two parts-*Avyakta* and evolutionary. The former with *Purusha* forms one category (*Avyakta*) while the latter part is called *Kshetra* (the former being *Kshetajana*)

But this sort of schism in unmanifested does not seem reasonable. Moreover, *Prakruti* cannot be *Kshetrajna* in any stage unmanifested. Perhaps *Dasgupta* has been led astray by *Chakrapani* who also seems to be confused. He interprets *'Avyakta'* as that which is natural from *Prakruti*

"अव्यक्तवर्जतिमतिप्रिकृत्युदासीनवर्जतिम्"

Further he adds that *Prakruti* is already conscious by the consciousness of natural *Purusha* or the indirectly conscious *Prakruti* as *Kshetrajna* Both sides to difficulties. In fact, on considering the context in entirety, it would be clear that the '*Avyakta'* of *Charaka* is different from that in *Isvarakrsna's Sankhya.* Here *'Avyakta'* denotes unequivocally the principle of consciousness (*Purusha*) and not *Prakruti* (the insentient matter). It is proved by *Charaka's* statements that the *'Avyakta'* is *Atma, Kshetrajna, Vibhu* and *Avyaya,* it has also been called as *Prakruti* (the final cause) and *Pradhana.* The epithets which are given to *Prakruti* in orthodox *Sankhya.* Thus *'Avyakta'* of *Charaka* is the only monarch of the situation and if the traditional *Prakruti* is to be adjusted it can be done only by taking the latter as *Shakti (*or *Maya)* of the lord[1]. This position is similar to that in *Gita* where lord is said as *Adhyaksha* and *Anumanta* of his own *Prakruti (Swayam Prakrutima).* As *Jiva* it becomes the part of the aggregate and is completely involved in the affair as fish in water forgetful of its real identity.

"नचतुर्वशिकोग्राह्योमनुजैर्ज्ञानदार्शभिः।

मत्स्यश्चोदकमन्वेतप्रिवर्तेतेप्रवर्तनात्।।

यथैवमत्स्यकृतथैषोअप्यवबुध्यते।"

-Mahabharat.Shanti.318.74-75

Because of this, in *Gita, Jiva* also is called as a sort of (*Para*) *Prakruti.* The *Para-atma* holds this conglomeration. *Chaturvinshatika, Panchvinshatika* and *Shadvinshatika* are, in fact, gradations of spiritual progress.

The term of *Shad-dhatuka Purusha* is found in the *Aatreya Aranyaka.* This was further confirmed by *Kakuda Katyayana* as said before. The three *Purusha's* of *Charaka* may be said as *Uttama, Madhyama* and *Prathama Purusha* which may be correlated with the same in *Gita* as *Purushottama, Aksara* and *Ksara* here also *Charaka* has taken the middle course and has accepted the *Madhyama*

Purusha (Shad-dhatuka) for practical purpose and which is said as *Karma Prurusha* by *Susruta.*

This main features of the *Sankhya Darshana* as given by *Charaka* are enumerated by Dasgupta. One point placed by him that the self is in itself unconscious cannot be agreed to. The statement of *Charaka* that the consciousness is released through its connection with senses does not mean that self is in itself without consciousness and depends for it on its instruments. The statement "*आत्माज्ञः*" clearly denotes that self-possesses consciousness. The word *"Sankhya"* is used in *Charaka Samhita* in which sense of philosophers rather than in limited senses of the orthodox *Sankhya Darshana*.

From the above description, it is known that Ayurveda and Philosophy have considered the *Atman* and *Purusha* is to be the same. Hence the description of the *Atman* is started.

***

CHAPTER-2

CONCEPT OF ATMAN

Substance and attributes are to be known (*Jneya*) and one who knowns or is acquainted with is called knower (*Jnata*). Soul is the substance which is knower.

Indian philosophy, Indian culture and Indian medical system are common in accepting the existence of soul, belief in destiny and in the consequence (good and bad) of action. Rebirth, almighty or supreme spirit and in another world *(Paraloka)* etc. lead towards theistic.

Charaka has condemned nihilism as nihilists don't believe in soul. For perception, soul is the essential factor. According to *Charak,* the empirical soul is endowed with the power of perception. Soul, mind ether, time and space are not ordinarily perceptible.

Western sciences, being generally based on the faith on the common laws of the nature in every walk of the life, try to define the life and universe on the known (generally material) factors of the nature. The empirical soul does not appear in the range of the study of modern materialistic science.

On the other hand, Ayurveda and other Indian systems do not accept the life, only as materialistic one. Ayurveda describes *Ayu* as a combination of body, sense organs, mind and soul. The entire worldly life depends on the combination of mind, soul and body. The combination likened to a tripod.

The similar is particularly significant. A tripod can sustain itself so long as none of its three constituents is disturbed imbalanced. The tripod in the present context constitutes the entire sentient beings. The belief in the existence of the soul clears this idea also that our present body is small particle of the ever-flowing stream of this great and gigantic universe. Our present life is result of our own past actions.

The formation of our future is also reserved in our own hand. Individual is the creator of his life. The acceptance of the consciousness as soul or almighty god also confirms our faith that one Omni conscious existence is present in the whole movable and unmovable as well as sentient and lifeless world.

This idea compiles a very important role in providing directions to our physical, mental and vocal activities. Ayurveda accepts three types of *Purusha* viz.

1. Absolute consciousness or *Parama Purusha*

2. Soul responsible for transmigration (*Ativahika Purusha*)

3. Empirical soul (*Rashipurusha* or *Sthola Chetna Sharira*)

These all divisions are based on the primary factor of the acceptance of soul. After accepting the soul, it clears that our present physical and mental development is the result of our previous actions and future will depend on the actions of this life.

***

CHAPTER-3

LIFE OF PRANA

Life of Prana-

Life has been a puzzle for all the beings. Ayurveda has tried to answer it. *Prana* is a term which is used as a very useful step in the descriptions of life. The conjunction of body with vital (*Prana*) is known as life *(Ayu)*. *Prana* is recognized by inspiration and expiration *(Prana & Apana)* as well as remain alive only till the vital exists in the body, hence, remaining physical structure is known as dead body.

The name of the person is given only when it is associated with vitae. When vitae transmigrate, it is generally said the person who was called by a specific name, it may be *Harisha, George* or *Abdullah,* has gone (to heaven or anywhere else) and the only cadaver is lying here.

Charaka, while defining the life, says that conjunction of body, sense organs, psyche and self-i.e. *(Atmana* or Vitae*)* is life (*Ayu*) and *Dhari, Jivita, Nityaga* and *Anubandha* are its synonyms. Continuance of consciousness *(Chetnanuvritti)* is cause and effect of the life. *Susruta* has mentioned twelve *Pranas* viz. *Agani, Soma, Vayu, Satva, Rajasa* and *Tamasa,* five sense organs (representatives of five *Mahabhutas*) and *Jivatma.* The *Atman* remains always with *Satva.*

The *Prana* originates from and is like the shadow of the *Purusha* comes in the body led by *Manasa. Doshas* are inherently related to *Prana* and are responsible for health and disease.

Atman as Padartha and Dravya

Padartha means the subject matter to be dealt with in a particular discipline are different, that is way the *Padarthas* of each discipline in *Nyaya* system and *Dravya* etc; six *Padarthas* have been described in *Vaisheshika* system.

In this reference *Satva, Atmana* and *Sharira* are the subject matter of Ayurveda. The body contains five elements and organs. Five elements and other constituents of the body are subject matter (*Padarthas*) category accepted in *Nyaya* system, and also accepted in Ayurveda.

Dravya is the substratum of property and action and is the material cause of its effect. They are nine viz., *Prithivi, Aap, Tejasa, Vayu, Akasha, Atmana, Manasa, Kala* and *Dika.*[21] *Atman* has got properties like respiration and other sentient symbols and the knowledge is its action. So, *Atman* is *Dravya* and is different from other substance and is most important for life.

Existence of Atman as described in Ayurveda

So many arguments have been placed in *Nyaya* system to prove the *Atman* factor different form sense organs which create confusion to be sentient. *Charaka* defining the practical aspect of this subject, says that all the sources of knowledge including scriptural, which serve as instrument for knowledge of various kinds, establish the causality of *Purusha.*

The bodily organs of a living being might be different but the soul i.e. the agent of action is one and the same. The agent of action like a sculptor is an efficient cause of all actions (viz. Sculpture etc.) by virtue of his possession of various instruments like *Vansi* and tongue.

The living being constantly undergo the process of destruction at a rate of faster than the twinkling of an eye. Regeneration of this ever-decrying phenomenon is impossible and results of the deeds *(like yajna)* of individual are not enjoyed by another individual.

In living beings, a factor other than the body (i.e. the soul) is responsible for ego, enjoyment of the fruits of action, engagement in action, transmigration and memory of action and it will not be possible to explain these points, unless the existence of a permanent entity known as *Purusha,* separate from the body is admitted.

The learned ones are therefore of the view that there is a permanent entity known as *Atman* or *Purusha,* who is the causative factor for the action as well as for the enjoyment of its fruits. *Samkhya* system also accepts their arguments.

***

CHAPTER-4

TYPES OF ATMAN

Two types of *Atman* have been described:

1. *Jivatma*

2. *Parmatma*

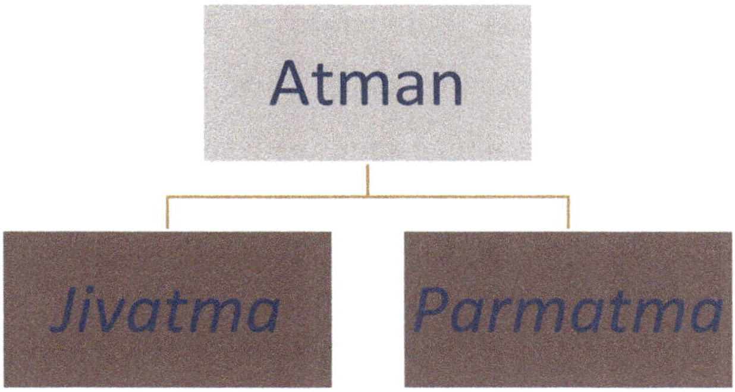

1. Jivatma

This type of *Atman* remains in each individual being. *Atman* is eternal, immutable, indivisible, and limitless and the base of consciousness. The properties of *Atman* are contrary to body.

The word *Sharira* itself meaning that which detritus every moment, indicates the destructive character of the body. The consciousness of the living being is due to soul, so it is called *Chetna Dhatu*.

Atman is free from disorders and transmutation (*Nirvikara*) whereas body and mind are prone to these. It is eternal (*Avinashi*). It is a continuum without any parts. It is omnipresent and as such cannot be limited to time and space whereas body and mind are limited. When all pervading *Jivatma* descends into embryo, the *Garbha* becomes conscious, on the other hand when *Atman* leaves the body the latter remains unconscious cadaver which is made of five elements.

Consciousness of *Atman* is manifested on contact with sense organs. The soul joined with body, mind and sense organs moves in different species is known as *Jivatman* and is recognised by the symptoms of life.

2.Parmatman

The absolute or supreme soul). It is beginning-less, no birth as such can be ascribed to him. It is faultless and so free from birth and death, loss or increase, free from *Rajasa* and *Tamasa,* and has got no attachment, enmity and sorrows. The physical body is known as *Kshetra* (corpus) and the unmanifested one is known as *Kshetragya* (knower of the corpus).

The body and mind constitute the substratum of disease and happiness. *Parmatman* or absolute consciousness is essentially devoid known as observer *(Drasta)*. The absolute soul cannot be perceived by anything, for eternity is not caused by anything, so the absolute soul is un-manifested and imperceptible.

The absolute soul is un-manifested (*Avyakta*) knower of creation (*Kshetragya*), eternal (*Shashvata*), universal (*Vibhu*) and indestructible (*Avyaya*). While the creation of the world can be perceptible through sense organs. The soul can be only inferred (rather than perceived).

Paramatman is known by so many names. Some of these names are. *Aksara.* (un-perishable and indestructible), *Jna* (the sentient soul), *Karta* (doer of all), *Purusha* (the Supreme Being, the soul, god-the soul of universe), *Chetana* (absolute consciousness), *Brhama* (the Supreme Being regarded as impersonal and divested of all qualities and action.

According to *Vedanta Darshan, Brahman* is both the efficient and the material cause of the visible universe, the all-pervading soul and spirit of the universe, the essence from which all created things are produced and into which they are absorbed.), *Sakshi* (observer or witness), *Karta* (doer), *Drasta* (viewer), *Vedita* and *Purushottama.*

Yoga Darshan describes *Ishwar* as a particular *Purusha* who is untouched by the affliction of life, actions, results and impressions produced by these actions.

Actually, all philosophical systems have given separate name to the supreme and almighty power and that is the same unmatchable God. The colour, taste, sound, hot or cold sensation and smell are properties which are grasped by sense organs, god has got no any such property so it cannot be grasped by any of the sense organ. In the same way, he does not possess happiness and sorrow etc. Attributes, so it can't be perceived by *Manasa.* Only self-experiences are the methods to known him.

***

Two types of Atman
have been described:
1. Jivatma
2. Parmatma
Jivatma
'Individual Soul"
Aspect of Atman that resides
within every living being and ex-
periences the cycle of birth, life,
deaift, and rebirth.
Parmatma
'Supreme Soul"
Absolute and universal aspect
of Atman that represents the inte
inrite and all-encompassing div-
ve consciousness.

CHAPTER-5

Five types of *Paramatman*

Bhutaman
Indriyatman
Pradhanatman
Jivatman
Paramatman

In *Vishnu Purana* the one soul has been described by five names, according to its different locations and conditions. On the other places also the single and one existence of the supreme power has been told in many and different methods.

The five types of *Atmana* are

1. *Bhutaman*
2. *Indriyatman*
3. *Pradhanatman*
4. *Jivatman*
5. *Paramatman*

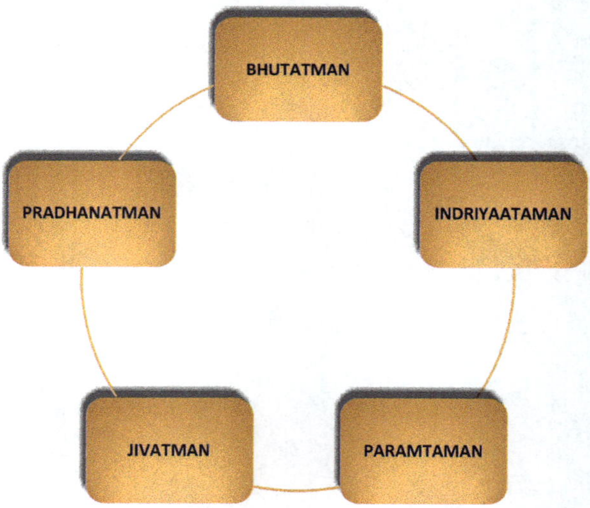

Bhutatman

The living being consists of five subtle elements (*Panca tanmatras*) and five gross elements (*Mahabhutas*). This body is called *Pura.* The *Atman* is called *Bhutatman* because it resides in the body which is formed with five elements called *Bhutas.*

It is an individual entity appose to the supreme soul. Due to the actions of consciousness the soul enters in the embryo with subtle elements. Soul, holding the body consist of five elements is called *Bhutataman. Linga sharira, Sukshma sharira* and *Bhutatman* are synonyms.

The soul can never dissociate himself from the trans-sensory and excessively subtle *Bhutas.* According to *Manusmruti,* the doer of the action is called *Bhutatman.* The empirical soul alone or *Bhutatman* (in the absence of instruments of knowledge and action) does neither initiates action nor enjoys the fruits of action. Thus, it is clear that the *Atman* associated with *Bhutas* is known as *Bhutatman.*

Indriyatma

The soul being free from all types of pathogenesis, projects its consciousness through sense organs. Due to attachment and even being dependent on *Indriyas* it is called *Indriyatma.*

Manasa is also an *Indriya* and the soul while shifting from one body to another, at the time of death and rebirth of one or another body, remains in close contact with *Manasa.*

Shushruta has used the terms such as *Sprsta* (one who touches), *Ghrata* (one who smells), *Drsta* (one who sees), *Rasayita* (one who receives the taste), and *Vakta* (one who speaks) etc. as synonyms of *Atman.*

Vakta indicates that other actions of *Karmendriyas* and also used to be done by soul. Thus, *Indriyas* and soul are interdependent and so being exposed through *Indriyas. Atma* is called as *Indriyatma.*

Pradhanatman

In philosophy the body is called *Kshetra* and the knower of the body is known as *Kshetragya. Kshetragya, Jna, Purusha* and *Atman* etc. are used as synonyms. The body *Manasa* and senses are conscious-less which *Atman* is conscious one, so he is known as *Karta.*

In all types of *Purushas* viz., *Ekdhatvika Purusha* (the supreme), *Sad-dhatvika Purusha, Ativahika Purusha* (soul responsible for transmigration), *Rashi Purusha* (empirical soul) or *Purusha* with 24 or 25 elements the soul or *Purusha* dominates all other factors so it is called *Pradhana.* Health and other achievements of the life are useless if the *Atman* is not present.

Samkhya system has given so many arguments in presence of *Purusha* and they all prove the importance of *Atman.* Thus being head and primary or *Pradhana* in all elements, it is called *Pradhanatma.*

It leads to salvation which is the ultimate goal of the life. The *Purusha* is the subject matter of Ayurveda and for this only the Ayurveda has brought it to light.

Jivatma

Jiva, indicates living and existence and *Jivana* synonyms life or *Ayush.* In this sense *Jivatman* means the individual soul enshrined in the human body. The *Sharira* itself means 'which deteriorates every moment', indicates the destructive character of the body.

On the contrary the soul is eternal, immutable, indivisible and limitless. It is the cause of consciousness and thought to be a part of supreme soul. It is the agent of action in the body. Soul cannot be perceived by any other sense except the Devine vision. He is omnipresent and can enter into any physique, can perform any action and can take any shape. He is beyond any sensory perception.

At the time of death, he leaves the previous body and enters into the foetus of new body. In the shape of subtle body (i.e. *Sukshma sharira* of *Samkhya*) *Jivatmas* are many in number and with each physical body, one *Jivatma* is attached.

Paramatman-

Supreme consciousness or absolute consciousness is known as *Parmatma.* He is one, beginning-less, eternal and omnipresent.

According to *Yogdarshana, Ishwar* is a particular *Purusha* who is untouched by the affection of life, actions and their results and impressions produced by these actions. He cannot be perceived by anything, for eternity it is not caused by anything.

The absolute soul is un-manifested and imperceptible. He is known as *Kshetragya.* The highest limits of omniscience remain in him. Being unconditioned by time he is teacher even of the ancients. He is cause of everything but nothing creates him. He is faultless and free from hate or attachment. He is the smallest from small and the largest from all the being and things. He sees without eyes and listens without ears.

The death and old age cannot affect him. He is enlightened with his own light like sun. No place remains vacant where. He is not present. It is clear with the previous description and references.

He (*Parmatma* or Absolute & supreme soul) is the base and cause of consciousness. As the same person, according to his actions is recognised and called with different names (like father, son, teacher etc.). So is with *Parmatman.*

***Jivatman* and its relation with *Parmatman*:**

Atman is of two types *Jivatman* and *Parmatman.*

Jivatman is thought to be a particle or shadow of supreme or absolute consciousness which is omnipresent, while *Jivatman* is limited to the particular body, where it is located for a particular life period.

Human being has got a developed infrastructure of mind, intellect and sense organs *Pragyaparadha* (intellectual blasphemy) is the cause of various diseases of the human beings and the aim of the life is to achieve the four goals of the life viz *Dharma* (to fulfil ones duties and to perform the virtuous acts), *Artha* (acquirement of wealth) *Kama* (gratification of desires) and *Moksha* (the final emancipation, liberation from the world, or salvation) To achieve these goals good health is required.

The *Moksha* is the ultimate aim of any *Jivatman*, as he wants to be finally associated with the Absolute soul. There are different methods to achieve the goal described by different systems of philosophies. *Gyana yoga*, *Karma yoga* and *Bhakti yoga* are the main ways which lead Jivatman (Empirical soul) towards *Parmatman* (Supreme soul).

Charaka Samhita, being a torch bearer of complete development of man, has got a clear vision regarding the complete health and absolute eradication of miseries *Charaka* describes that desires are the root cause of miseries.

A silkworm provides for itself suicidal threads, so does an ignorant person, bound with worldly miseries, provides for himself desires arising out of the various objects. A wise person, who obtains from the objects of senses considering them as dangerous as burning fire, does not subject himself to any wishful act and contacts with there objects with the results that miseries never overcome him. Discussing about the eradication of miseries, it is essential to know the causes of miseries.

Impairment of intellect. patience and memory, advent of the maturity (of the results) of time and action and unwholesome contact with the objects of senses are considered to be the causative factors of miseries as intellectual blasphemy aggravate all the *Doshas*.

According to Ayurveda types of Atmana

Types of Atmana

The science of life (Ayurveda) is brought to light for the sake of *Purusha* and the *Purusha* as described by Ayurveda is the combination of mind, soul and body. These three are like a tripod and the word is sub-stained by their combination.

The *Purusha* is sentient and this is the subject matter of *Veda* (Ayurveda). The trio of *Sharira, Manasa* and *Atma* has got 24 (25 as per *Samkhya*) elements is known as *Purusha* and action, fruits of action, knowledge, ignorance happiness, misery, life, death and ownership are established in it.

Those who are interested to learn medical science must know about all the 24 elements which are responsible for life. The soul is regarded as a cause of creation. It means if *Purusha* were not there, nothing would happen.

Here one thing must be remembered that some other types of medical sciences may do not accept the existence of soul but in an ideal health Ayurveda accepts the happiness of *Atma* as an essential factor actually medical science has got no use if the combination of five elements and soul is not presented for the treatment. Soul without five elements or *Sharira* does not need any treatment and the *Sharir* from which the soul has gone; being called dead body, cannot be treated. Sympathy is the important factor of any pathy of treatment and without sympathy all the patients are useless.

The sympathy is the quality available only in living and culture organism. Thus, the Ayurvedic view point is very important, useful and practically fruitful to all concerned.

Three types of *Atma* and *Purusha* have been described in Ayurveda viz.-

1. *Parmatma* or *Param Purusha*
2. *Ativahika Purusha* or *Sukshama Sharira*
3. *Sthoola Chetan Purusha* or *Karma Purusha*

***Parmatma* (the absolute soul):**

No body requires disease as it is an obstacle and causes the distraction of *Manasa* the body and mind constitute the substrata of disease and happiness (i.e. positive health).

The soul is absolutely detached of all the bodily and psychological aliments. Of course, soul causes consciousness through the agency of the mind the specific qualities of the basic elements (*Mahabhutas*) as well as sense organs. Where ever the agency (mind and body) is not available, no consciousness is manifested. The soul observes all activities. In worldly practice, only the knower is recognised as witness. All attributes, actions, etc. of *Bhutas* are witnessed by soul, who alone is knower of all things.

Things cannot be witnessed by unconscious objects like stone. Soul is beginning less, omnipresent and all pervasive. The absolute soul is one only and he is inaccessible by any signs and symptoms. He is un manifested, knower of creation, eternal, universal and imperceptible.

The term *Purusha* is also used for the personalities comprised from six or twenty-four elements, in this sense the cows and goats, etc. (all living beings) may be called

Purusha without any difference of gender etc, but the term generally refers to human being who dominates all. Even then element of consciousness alone constitutes *Purusha.*

Ativahika or _Linga Sharira_ (Soul responsible for transmigration):

The concept of soul with subtle body called as *Ativahika Purusha* or *Linga Sharira* has been accepted in Ayurveda. This type of soul is responsible for transmigration of *Jiva* from one body to another. It is a permanent common question before every thinker that how does the soul transmigrates from one body to another and with who it is always attached.

Indian philosophers have described this matter in many ways. According to *Charaka,* being guided by the associated past actions, the soul who travels with the help of the mind, transmigrates from one body to another along with the four subtle elements viz. *Prithivi, Jala, Agni* and *Vayu,* this *Sukshma Sharira* cannot be perceived by any other sense except the divine version. He is omnipresent and can enter into any physique, can perform any action and can take any shape.

The association of subtle bodies with the sperm an ovum; is conditioned by the actions of past life. The colour of the cloth is dependent on the colour of threads composing the cloth. Similarly, the characteristic features of the gross body resemble these of the subtle body. Not only the physique but also the mental faculties of the individual resemble those of the subtle body. Action like charity, study, meditation, etc in the past life give the individual a *Satvika* type of mind.

Depending upon the past actions, the soul may enter into the body of any species, viz. human being, animals, etc. of *Rajasa* and *Tamasa* variations and the actions of past life are responsible for the variations in the characteristic features of individuals.

According to *Acharya Kapila* of *Samkhya Darshana Linga Sharira* consist of 17 elements viz. *Buddhi,* 10 *Indriyas, Manasa* and five *Tanmatras. Samkhya karika* includes *Mahan, Ahamkara, Manasa, 10 Indriyas* and five elements i.e. 18 elements in *Sukshma Sharira.* These *Linga Shariras* are produced separately for each being and cannot utilise the worldly fruits of his action without gross body.

As the shadow cannot remain without a tree etc. or a picture cannot be imagined without its establishment like paper etc, so the subtle body cannot remain or act without gross body.[68] This subtle body moves from one body to another, to enjoy the fruits of it, actions as a black bee, movies from one flower to another to enjoy the taste. He moves till he is not liberated.

***Rashi Purusha* or *Sthula Chetana Sharira* (empirical soul):**

Tied up and limited with death and birth, the gross body is called *Sthula Chetana Purusha.* It is also called *Kshetra* which is the residing point of *Kshetagya* or soul. The word *Sharira* itself meaning, which deteriorates every moment, indicates the destruction character of the body. The synonyms used for body is *Deha* and *Kaya* denote the growth aspect of body which also ends in destruction. The body is destructible, changeable, divisible and limited mass of five elements or *Bhutas*.

It has been so many nomenclatures according to its composition or activity.

The main synonyms are *Rashipurusha, Karmapurusha, Samyogapurusha* and *Chaturvinshatika purusha* etc. The qualities defined by these terms are-

Chikitsiya Purusha-

The *Purusha* is like a tripod, consists of mind, soul and body, is sentient and is the subject matter of Ayurveda. Being the subject matter of *Chikitsa,* the body is called *Chikitsiya purusha.*

Karma purusha-

All the actions are performed by this and even all the actions are performed for the shake of this, so it is called *Karmapurusha.* The action, the fruit of action, knowledge, ignorance, happiness, miseries, life and ownership are established here.

Samyoga purusha-

Manasa, soul and body combine or contact together in this, so this is called *Samyoga purusha.* For these sensations do not constitute of attributes of soul as such. They infect arise out of the contacts of the sense organs with their objects.

Rashipurusha* or *Chaturvinshatika purusha-

According another classification, *Purusha* is comprised with 24 *Dhatus,* i.e *Manasa,* 10 *Indriyas,* 5 objects of sense organs, and *Prakruti* viz. 5 *Mahabhutas, Ahamkara, Mahana* and *Avyakta.* According to the *Samkhya* system of philosophy, *Purusha* constitutes the 25 elements. In the description accepted by *Acharya Charaka, Purusha* has been included under *Prakrti.*

As the supreme Soul is beginingless, no birth as such can be ascribed to Him. Of course, the empirical soul (*Puruşa*), who represents the com- bination or collection of 24 elements (here by called *Rasi Purusa*) is born out of action prompted by liking and dislikings originated from ignorance.

To establish the separate identity from absolute consciousness (*Parama Purusha*) and soul responsible for transmigration (*Ativahika Purusha*), the empirical soul has been described by various names viz. *Sthula Sharira* (gross body), *Karma purusha, Rasipurusha, Samyoga Purusha* and *Caturvinstika Purusha.* No doubt the evolution of the entire universe can be included in the empirical soul or *Rasi purusha*, as each and every thing comes in this preview, but here in the medical science (Ayurveda) only human being is accepted as *Purusha.*

The previous two types of *Purusha* viz *Parama Purusha* and *Ativahika* or *Suksma Shari*ra, being free from the gross body, neither do any work nor can enjoy the fruits of their actions. Their treatment is also not possible in the absence of gross physical body. So, the empirical soul or *Cikitsya Purusha* is accepted as the aim of Ayurveda.

Sr.	PURUSH	DHATU	SAMKHYA	SYNONYMS
1	EK DHATUJ PURUSH	CHETNA	1	-
2	SHAD DHATUJ PURUSH	PANCHMAHA BHUT + AATMA	6	KARMA PURUSH CHIKITSHYA PURUSH
3	CHATURVINS HATI PURUSH	MAN+10 INDRIYA+5 ARTH+ASHT PRAKRUTI	24	-RASHI PURUSH - SAMYOG PURUSH

***

CHAPTER-6

PROPERTIES OF ATMAN

PARMATMA - PROPERTIES AND EVIDENCE OF THE ABSOLUTE SOUL
According to Charaka Samhita
Properties of Parmatma
1. Samkhya - Number One
2. Parimana - Vibhu (All-Pervading)
3. Prithakatva - Distinctness
4. Samyoga - Conjunction with Body
5. Vibhaga - Separation at Death
6. Iccha - Divine Will
7. Prayatna - Effort / Motivation
8. Buddhi - Supreme Intellect
8. Buddhi - Supreme Intellect
8. Buddhi - Supreme Intellect
Evidence of the Existence of the Absolute Soul
(Signs Mentioned in Charaka Samhita)
1. Prana & Apana - Inspiration & Expiration
2. Twinkling of the Eyes
3. Life
4. Material Perception
4. Shift of Sense Objects
5. Mobility & Stability of Mind
7. Journey in Dreams
7. Journey in Dreams
9. Cross-Visual Cognition (Right → Left Eye)
10. Desire and Hatred
11. Happiness and Misery
12. Effort and Consciousness
13. Stability and Intellect
14. Memory and Ego
Soul as the Source of Life, Consciousness and Awareness

Atman is the base where the knowledge is located. *Atma* does not have the qualities like colour, shape, taste and touching sensation. So, it cannot be perceived by sense organs. The existence of knower cannot be perceived by senses.

It is the examination of corporal body and its particular functions that guide whether the knower (*Atma*) exists or not. If knower alone is cognized it is called *Kaivalya,* the highest achievement. *Atma* is therefore the distinct feature of living beings than the examinable body. But it should be noted that simple movement is not suggestive of entity of *Atma.*

Properties of *Parmatman-*

As already discussed, the *Atman* or consciousness is one and has been described of two types. The consciousness confined to one physical body is known as *Jivatma* and is recognized by several symptoms as well as properties and when *Jivatma* leaves the body, only five elements remain like the empty house. The consciousness or *Parmatma* has the following properties.

1. *Samkhya* (number-one)
2. *Parimana* (measurement-*Vibhu*)
3. *Prthakatva*
4. *Samyoga*
5. *Vibhaga*

6. *Iccha*

7. *Prayatna*

8. *Buddhi*

Symptoms and properties of *Atman-*

Atman are known as the base of cognition or knowledge. So many signs and symptoms have been described in different references of Ayurveda and philosophical texts. Consciousness or presence of *Jivatma* is acknowledged by these symptoms and the existence of *Atman* is experienced due to these symptoms. According to *Charaka Samhita* the existence of the absolute soul.

1. *Prana & Apana* (inspiration and expiration)
2. Twinkling of the eyes
3. Life
4. Material perception
5. Shift from one object of sense organ to another
6. Mobility and stability of mind
7. Journey to another place in dream
8. Anticipation of death
9. Knowledge of something visualized in the right eye by the left eye
10. Feelings of desire
11. Hatred
12. Happiness

13. Misery
14. Effort
15. Consciousness
16. Stability
17. Intellect
18. Memory
19. Ego

Susruta has also described these properties. This description resembles to that of *Vaisheshika Darshana* where the marks of the existence of soul have been described viz. the ascending life breath (*Prana*), the descending life breath (*Apana*), the closing and opening of the eyes (*Unmesha* and *Nimesha*), the movement of the mind and the affections of the other senses, and also pleasure, pain, desire, aversion and effort.

Thus, it can be imagined that cognition is the mark of soul and the combination of soul and body (where the soul resides) is recognized by these symptoms. Soul is a substance and eternal. The soul is really proved by revelation or by realization only and it could be proved by reasoning or by inference, since visible and commonly observed marks do not exist in it.

***

CHAPTER-7

EXISTENCE

OF

THE SOUL

The soul is the ruler
of body and universe
Theists
(Astika)
Consciousness
requires a soul
VS
Nihilists &
Atheists
(Nastika)
No such substance
exists

The soul is called ruler or governor of all factors of the body as well as of the universe. The theist (*Astika*) school of philosophers accepts it and, in their view, it is essential for consciousness.

On the other hand, the nihilist and atheists (*Nastika*) do not believe in the existence of any such substance. According to them, the consciousness appears not due to any such factor like soul but it is only due to the combination of some factors and the consciousness available in the body is due to mind and senses only, no any other substance like soul is required.

The existence or non-existence of the soul has been the question of discussion for all times; Ayurveda believes in theism and condemns the nihilism as it constitutes worst of sinful.

Charaka while discussing three basic desires of life the third desire has been described as desire for happiness in future life (*Parlokaisana*). This desire is in-fact shrouded with some doubts. There is a doubt, whether one will have a life (rebirth) at all, after his death. Due to its imperceptibility, it should not be accepted.

Charaka answers that the scope of perception is very limited. Even the sense faculties, throw which one can perceive of objects, themselves are not the objects of direct perception. Moreover, it is not correct to say that only things which can be directly perceived exist and others do not.

The existing things cannot be directly perceived due to over proximity, over distance, obstruction, weakness of senses, diversion of mind, confusion with other similar objects, over shadowing and over minuteness.

Charaka further says that *Atman*, the sustainer of consciousness is eternal and cannot be created by anything else. If creation by something else refers to the creation of the body by the absolute *Atman*, this would be an acceptable view.

The views of nihilists regarding accidental (*Yadriccha*) are not acceptable, as for a nihilist there is nothing to examine and the existence of examiner also do not exist. The acceptance of this theory may create humbug in universe.
The means for getting the correct knowledge is known as *Pramana*. Everything can be divided into two categories true and untrue or existing and non-existing. These can be

examined by taking recourse to one of the following four methods viz.

Aptopdesa (scriptural testimony), *Pratyaksha* (direct observation) *Anumana* (inference) and *Yukti* (reasoning). All the four means of knowledge establish the theory of rebirth and thus the existence of soul has been also established.

Some persons believe that life can be created only by the virtue of combining different organs. Answering this *Charaka* asks how a pitcher or any other pot can be constructed inspite of earth, rod, wheel etc, if there is no potter? Can a house be constructed inspite of the earth, straw beams etc, if there is no mason? Certainly not. Then how can the life (living body) can be created without a conscious agent. Those who believe and think on these lines are devoid of rational outlook.

Some other philosophers (mainly Buddhists) believe in the theory of momentary existence of things. Here is another question that when the things present at one moment are destroyed on the second moment, where and how the knowledge will remain. According to them the results of action performed by one would be enjoyed by some other monetary entities who have not performed the actions.

Emphasizing on the existence of *Purusha*, *Charaka* further says that the bodily organs of a living being might be different but the soul is one and the same.

If, for a moment it is accepted that consciousness and power to act remains is physical body, the questions arise, why it does not appear in a dead body, where everything except *Prana* remains the same as it was previous to the death.

On this ground it is essential to search a separate agency responsible for consciousness in addition to body, sense organs and manes. If body is accepted as the seat of consciousness, it is worth remembering that the cells and tissues of different parts of the body such as blood, muscular tissue and even brain tissues are passing through a process of bear and tear and the new tissues replace the old one. Actually, it is the process of life.

A child cumulates knowledge on different topic in his early age. In his youth and elder age, most of the tissues of the body as well as organs are changed. If the cells or tissue of the senses are thought to be the seat of knowledge, the knowledge collected in child hood, must be destroyed in later ages. But practically an old man uses his bunch of knowledge and experience which was gained in his early age.

This proves that the seat of knowledge i.e. soul is definitely different from the body. Some philosophers argue that eye, ear etc. senses organs. Collect the knowledge directly, so, they must be recognized as a seat of knowledge.

But here is one problem. When, in an accident any of the sense organ is lost, suppose a man becomes blind. If the eyes were considered as a seat of knowledges, definitely all the previous knowledge must have been lost. But practically it is experienced that by missing of the eyes etc., the old experiences are not missed. It proves that the seat of the knowledge is separate from sense organs and this is known as soul.

Manasa can also not be accepted as the seat of knowledge, because it is also an instrument of the knowledge like other senses. It is somehow superior and more powerful than other sense organs but no doubt it is an *indriya*. If *Manasa* is thought to be a conscious agency, the happiness and misery etc. will not be acknowledged as mana is atomic in measurement.

Manasa is an instrument and unconscious and so it cannot be doer and knower. The existence of doer always differs from instrument. The ruler and governor of all these factors is soul. *Nyaya* system has also accepted it. Writing is an action; pen the instrument of writing is totally different from writer.

In the same way, the instrument of knowledge i.e. *Indriyas* and *Manas* cannot do the act of knowing. Knower, the seat of consciousness and knowledge is soul and it has a separate existence.

Soul-its singularity of plurality:

After accepting the existence of soul, one more important question arises regarding the number of souls. Whether it is one authority two types viz. *Parmataman* and *Jivataman* of soul have been accepted. The *Parmataman* (the Absolute and Supreme God) is one, while the *Jivatmans* are numerous and remain separately in each living body.

Charaka Samhita describes that being guided by associated past actions, the soul with the help of manas travels to the different bodies. He is omnipresent and can enter into any physique; can perform any action and can take any shape. The dissimilarities in the shape and intellectual faculties is caused by *Rajas*, *Tamas* and the nature of the past actions.

The separate actions of separate being at separate timings prove the numerous characters of *Jivatman*. *Samkhya* system of philosophy advocates that the birth and death of the different beings in the universe take place at different times, all the persons do not do the same work at the same time and the three attributes viz. *Rajasa*, *Tamasa* and *Satva* present the different aspects of mental faculties in different persons at the same time, are the reasonings in favour of many *Jivatmans*.

According to this system of thought, if there would have been only singular number of souls, all the persons (beings) must be taking birth or dying at a particular time. In the same way all the persons would have sleeping, eating, hearing etc. simultaneously.

But practically it does not happen. We see that in one family the persons are waiting for new guest and at the same time the others are preparing to see off one of his beloved family members for eternity. The absence of similar activities at a time shows the numerousness of the *Jivatamans*.

It is also seen that some persons are going through anger endowed with *Rajasa* passion, some for greed while other are reaching some *Satvika* approached like devotion. This pattern shows that *Jivatmans* are numerous and one soul is present in each living creature.

Soul and its tendency towards knowledge:

The mind, intellect, cognitive and cognitive organs are the instruments of knowledge. Their association with the doer (Empirical soul) results in action, sensation and understanding. Here, the question arises that when soul is called '*Jna*' or knower, why he is not the knower at all times and why the help of different instruments like *Manas* and sense organs is required?

Charaka Samhita on this point clears that the empirical soul is endowed with the power of perception. It perceives things when it is associated with the mind, intellect and sense faculties. In the absence or impedance of these instruments, the perception cannot take place.

One cannot get the real reflected picture of an image from a mirror which is covered with dirt or from water which is muddy. Similarly, when the mind etc. gets afflicted, the perception does not appear.

***

CHAPTER-8

LOKA-PURUSA SAMYA

Lok Purusha-Samya Siddhant
(Microcosm-Macrocosm Doctrine)
लोक
पुरुष

The relations of individuals (*Jivatman*) and universe (*Parmatman*) are well described in *Puruşavicaya Sharira* chapter of *Charaka samhita* that an individual is an epitome of the universe.

Realisation of the fact that attachment leads to miseries and detachment to happiness is the real knowledge. So, moving in the state of confusion caused by the turmoil of the dosas like *Ahmakara*, he cannot overcome attachment, which is the root cause of all evils.

On the other hand, detachment is salvation. It is *Para* (Absolute) and *Prasanta* (serene). It is *Aksara* (Immutable). It is *Brahman*. It is *Moksa* (emancipation). In this reference, *Charaka* has described the ways and means of getting salvation and concluded the list of these methods with the comment that in vitiated mind gets purified by their purifying factors as a (dirty) mirror is cleaned with help of oil, cloth and hair etc.

As the solar disc dazzles when it is not covered by *Rahu*, cloud, dust smoke and fog, so does the mind shine when it is in the state of purity.

As the *Rahu* etc. five factors are thought to create obstruction in the brilliance of the sun, so the five sense organs may obstruct the purity of mind. Describing the process and method of adopting the salvation, *Charaka* says that a person with his mind pure, is in possession of true wisdom (*Sataya-buddhi*) which expels the excessively thick darkness caused by ignorance, which brings about detachment and knowledge about the nature of all things.

Which is conductive to attainment of *Yogic* power; which renders the individual wise, which brings about freedom from variety and detachment from the causative factors of miseries, which renders the individual free from hopes, which brings about renunciation and which serves as a means to attainment of Brahman, the eternal, immutable, tranquil and indestructible.

It is this wisdom which is known as *Vidya* (learning), *Siddhi* (accomplishment), *Mati* (wisdom) *Medha* (power of retention), *Pragya* (intellect) and *Gyana* (knowledge). By the development of true wisdom (*Satya buddhi*) all the desires are eliminated. Each empirical soul or *Jivatma* is trying to dissolve himself with Supreme soul.

This condition is called *Shanti* (liberation), *Vipapa* (free from sinful acts), *Viragya* (free from attachments), *Santa* (serene), *Para* (absolute), *Aksara* (indestructible), *Avyaya* (immutable), *Amrta* (immortal), *Brahman* (god) and *Nirvana* (the state of extinction of all miseries).

By this spiritual knowledge the stage of *Prasama* (absolute tranquility or unlimited happiness) i.e salvation is attained which is the only and ultimate goal of each Jivatma.

***

LOKAGATA BHAVA - PURUSHGATA BHAVA

Cosmic and Human Factors Connection

Sr. No.	Lokgata Bhava (Universe Factors)	Purushgata Bhava (Body entities)
1.	Prithvi	Murti (Shape and Appearance)
2.	Apa (Kleda and Moisture)	Kleda (Fluid and Moisture)
3.	Tejas Heat / Digestion	Abhisantapa (Heat, Hotness, Burning Sensation)
4.	Vayu	Prana ayu (Liveliness)
5.	Viyat (Akasha)	Sushira (Tissues or Free spaces)
6.	Brahma	Antaratma (Inner Rulling Mechanism)
7.	Vibhuti of Brahmi Inner Rulling Mechanism)	Vibhuti of Antaratma Vibhuti of Antaratma
8.	Prajapati	Sattva (Mind)
9.	Indra	Ahankara (Ego)
10.	Aditya	Adana (to make grahana)
11.	Rudra	Rosha (Anger)
12.	Soma	Prasada (Happiness)
13.	Vasu	Kanti (Lustre)
14.	Ashwini Kumara	Utsaha (Wish to work)
15.	Marut	Indriya (All Sense Organs)
16.	Vishwadeva	Moha (Darkness)
17.	Tamo	Jnana (Knowledge)
18.	Sargaadi	Garbhadana (Conception)
19.	Krita yuga	Balya-avastha (Childhood)
20.	Treta yuga	Vriddha awastha (Youth)
21.	Kali yuga	Aturavastha (Diseases)
24.	Yuganta kala	Mrityu (Death)

Theism & Remembering of God and Ayurveda:

Two types of philosophical schools viz. theist and atheist have been developed by the thinkers. To have faith in rebirth, Vedas, soul and almighty is theism. Ayurveda believes in theism and has condemned the nihilism, as it is worst of the sinful acts. So, a wiseman should however give up the heterodox view and related doubts.

Bhagvadgita accepts five essential factors for the success of any activity viz, establishment, doer, instruments, action and deity. Ayurveda being a theist system has accepted and described the utility of various ritual actions and to recollect different names of God as well as *Mantras* very useful for health. Therapies are off three kinds viz.

spiritual therapy, therapy based on reasoning (physical propriety) and psychic therapy. Spiritual therapies are incantation of mantras, talisman, wearing of gems, auspicious offerings, gifts, oblations, observance of scriptural rules, atonement, fasts, chanting of auspicious hymns, obeisance to the gods and pilgrimage etc.

Spiritual therapies have empirical powers to eradicate diseases instantaneously. Such therapies are, as a matter of fact, related to the blessings and influence of the God. All the items numerated here are effective in eradication of disease only due to divine influence.

The role of *Isvara* has been accepted even before the life of an individual starts. While entering into cohabitation with a desire of child, incantation of *Mantras* should be recited. *Charaka* has quoted some Vedic rites for procreating a child of desired qualities.

A *Mantra* from *Rigveda* was used for this purpose. For painless and faultless delivery, *Vishnu* (the second deity of the sacred *Triad-Brhama-Vishnu-Mahesha* entrusted with the preservation of world, which duty He is represented to have duly discharged by his various incarnations which are called *Avtaras*.) was remembered.

In K*ashyapa Samhita* references about *Tripurari Mahadeva, Rudra, Bhutesvara, Neelkantha* and *Vrsabhadhwaja* (all synonyms to lord *Sankara*) are available in various references.

Kalpasthana of *Charaka*, in the reference of using the medicine, indicates that the cup filled with the drug should be enchanted with a hymen meaning *Brahma Daksha,*

Ashwina, Rudra, Indra, earth, moon, sun, air, fire, sages, medicinal plants and multitude of creatures may protect you. The collection of the medicines should be done after worshipping deities and *Ashwins-twins*.

According to *Charaka* one, worshipping to Lord *Shiva* along with *Parvati*, congregation of mothers and their attendants is relieved quickly of intermittent fever.

One is free from all types of fever by eulogizing *Visnusahasranama* (Thousand names of lord *Visnu*) who is thousand headed master of all mobile and immobile creations of the world, and omnipresent with thousands of names.

One overcomes fever by worshipping with sacrifices *Brahma, Ashwins, Indra, Agni, Himalaya*, *Ganga* and congregations of *Marutas*.

Some sayings are famous in Indian society which indicate that the remembrance of *Isvara* was very common as its therapeutic use. These and many other references from different Ayurvedic literature show their support to theism. Here, *Brahma* is thought to be the creator of the whole creation (world) and the same *Brahma* is remembered as propounder of Ayurveda.

Ayurveda was developed from *Atharvaveda*. All those systems, who believe in Vedas, rebirth and soul etc; are called theist. Ayurveda believes all these, so it is a theist system.

From the above description it can be said that the soul is responsible factor for the origin of *Purusha* and their diseases. Hence the description of ***Atmavaad*** is started that is mentioned in *Yajjapurushiya Adhyaya Sambhasha*--

Pariksha, a descendant of *Mudgala*, having examined it said, that the living being originates from the soul and so the diseases also originate from the soul; thus, it is the soul which is the root cause of living beings and their diseases.

The soul alone collects and enjoys the actions and their results respectively. Happiness (that is freedom from diseases) and miseries (that is affliction with diseases) can never occur without the soul.

The following questions are answered in this verse:

1. What is the origin of living beings and diseases?
2. Is the origin of both of them the same?

How to ascertain that the origin of living beings and their diseases is the same? It is the soul which is responsible for collecting all actions which in their turn cause diseases or otherwise.

This *Sambhasha* will be continued in *Satvavaad*............

***

Bibliography

S. No	Book Name	Author Name	Publication	Edition
1	*Ayurveda Ke 6 Dashak*	Prof. Satyadev Dubey & Dr. Anugrah Narayan Singh	Chaukhamba Surbharti Prakashan, Delhi	1st Ed., 2005
2	*Charak Samhita: Ayurveda Dipika Ayushi Hindi Commentary*	Prof. Banvari Lal Gaud (Editor-Translator)	RAV, Delhi	1st Ed., 2011
3	*A History of Indian Philosophy*	Surendranath Dasgupta	Rupa Publications India Pvt. Ltd., New Delhi	2018
4	*Sushrut Samhita: Nibandha Sangraha Hindi Commentary*	Dr. Keval Krishna Thakaral (Editor-Translator)	Chaukhanbha Orientalia Publication, Varanasi	Reprint Ed., 2016

5	*Padartha Vijnana*	Prof. Dr. Yogesh Chandra Mishra	Chaukhamba Sanskrit Bhavan, Varanasi	Reprint Ed., 2005
6	*Shrimad Bhagavad Gita*	Maharaj Shrishrimadb haktivedant Narayan Goswami	Naveen Krishna Brahmachari Vidyalankar Publication, Mathura	1st Ed., 1997
7	*Charaka Samhita: Chakrapani Datta's Ayurveda Dipika English Translation & Critical Exposition*	Dr. Ram Karan Sharma & Vaidya Bhagwan Dash (Editor-Translator)	Chowkhamb a Sanskrit Series Office, Varanasi	Reprint Ed., 2018

www.ingramcontent.com/pod-product-compliance
Ingram Content Group UK Ltd.
Pitfield, Milton Keynes, MK11 3LW, UK
UKHW021403190726
13845UKWH00028B/852

9 789357 592963